Sonnets.

Charles Strong

991 к 31

SONNETS.

SONNETS.

BY

REV. CHARLES STRONG, A. M.

FORMERLY FELLOW OF WADHAM COLLEGE, OXFORD,

AUTHOR OF " SPECIMENS OF SONNETS FROM THE MOST CELEBRATED
ITALIAN POETS, WITH TRANSLATIONS."

LONDON :

JOHN MURRAY, ALBEMARLE-STREET.

MDCCCXXXV.

LONDON :
BRADBURY AND EVANS, PRINTERS, WHITEFRIARS.
(LATE T. DAVISON.)

TO

THE EARL OF HARROWBY,

THE FOLLOWING

SONNETS

ARE RESPECTFULLY INSCRIBED,

BY

HIS OBLIGED SERVANT,

THE AUTHOR.

TORQUAY, MAY 4, 1835.

RAISED, like a jewelled trophy, in mid-sky
Orion shone, Jove's star o'erhung the West,
Eastward, in all her beauty early drest,
Venus proclaim'd the conquering Sun was nigh:

Thousands of nameless Worlds stood glittering by;
And myriads, streaming far beyond the rest
From Heaven's low circuit to the polar crest,
Were seen, through optic tube, by wondering eye:

Nor yet unmarshalled, like a routed Host,
In shining multitudes at random driven,
Crowd they thro' some interminable coast;

All, in the regions infinite of Heaven,
In their appointed course, as Thou, Lord, know'st,
Obey the voice of Thy command—once given.

II.

ON PRESENTING THE LORD PRESIDENT OF THE COUNCIL WITH "SPECIMENS OF
ITALIAN SONNETS WITH TRANSLATIONS."

AMONG the titles which thy worth commend
To Fame's bright record, and the World's esteem,
First to the grateful Muse, and dearest, seem
The gifted Scholar and the Patron-friend:

'Tis thus invoked she woos thee to suspend
All graver cares, and, by the Tuscan stream,
In shades romantic wrapt, indulge the dream,
Which to their votary's prayer the Sisters lend.

Scipio and Lælius, as pleased Marcus tells,
Would oft, when Senates closed, the hours beguile,
Pacing the yellow sands in quest of shells.

Now England's course is smooth, and no cloud lowers,
Quit, noble HARROWBY, the helm awhile,
And stoop to Poesy's minuter flowers.

III.

Ye Stars of Heaven, that, through the veil of Night,
Look mercifully down, ah! gaze ye not,
With pity, on this dark sublunar spot,
Whose good so soon was marred by evil's blight?

Perchance, within your spheres' unfading light,
Immortal Beings hold a godlike lot;
Who never the command divine forgot,
Nor feared their Maker's voice, nor shunned his sight:

Or, are ye stationed in the wilds of space
To welcome those, who Death have overthrown,
And fit their vision for the blissful place?

From glory on to glory fuller shown
Our Guides, till we behold Him face to face,
And, in His likeness, know as we are known.

IV.

To this fair Island, in the western sea,
From green Devonia's vales I came—to die;
In vain the fondest care, serenest sky,
Long had gone forth th' immutable decree:

Long had I been resigned—Ye, only, Ye,
Who watched my slow decline with anxious eye,
To Earth still bound me with affection's tye;
For Love made known what sorrow yours would be:

Yet mourn not—All the shadowy scene must leave
At morn or noon, ev'n those, who stay awhile,
Count but a few brief hours, and sink at eve:

Like Israel's Prince resume your wonted style;
Ye cannot doubt my bliss, ye may not grieve,
Whilst in your memory lives my DYING SMILE.

V.

THOUGH Alps in awful grandeur stood around,
With all the wonders their deep bosoms hold,
Summer's bright verdure, snow's eternal cold,
Dark pine-clad steeps, and torrent-gulf profound;

Still, like the Pilgrim, on sweet errand bound,
Whose eyes with passing glance the scenes behold,
Which realms of beauty to his view unfold,
I sped with eager step tow'rds Latian ground:

My fancy lingered round the imperial halls,
Where she had made herself a shadowy home,
By Tiber's banks, and Anio's waterfalls:

My childhood's thought, my youth's desire, was Rome:
Strangely I longed to walk within her walls,
And worship God beneath his proudest dome.

VI.

CHIEF of the giant mountains! awful form!
Alp! on whose brow, wreathed with eternal snows,
Suns smite in vain, when radiant summer glows,
And harvests ripen through thy valleys warm;

Oft I behold thee girdled with the storm,
Oft, when the Moon her quiet splendour throws
O'er thy vast solitudes, and darkly shows
The scars and ruins which thy sides deform.

Thy summit pure, so free from earthly stain,
Seems meet approach to that immortal state
Where peace unclouded holds her starry reign:

The Few who climb thee, with strange joy elate,
Thus mingling with the skies, forget their pain,
Like Pilgrims fresh-arrived at heaven's own gate.

VII.

Ocean! I love thee in thy boisterous mood,
When thy strong billows wrestle with the land,
Or, with high crest careering o'er the strand,
Leap the dark cliff, and scare the sea-bird's brood:

I love thee, Ocean, when by Zephyr woo'd
Thy placid waters tremblingly expand,
And his soft whisper greet with smiles, as bland
As thy face wore, when God first call'd thee good.

Yet most I love thee, when, from low-browed cave,
I watch, as sheds the Moon the golden path,
That leads to heaven across thy slumbering wave:

But I abhor thee, when, in senseless wrath,
Thou swallowest up the gentle, and the brave,
In sight of home, and friends, that throng to save.

VIII.

BEAUTY! when intellectual charms are thine,
And kindling features eloquently speak
Soft sensibility, and temper meek,
I fondly turn, and worship at thy shrine;

But when these gifts, that make thee all divine,
Ennoble not the soul, nor bloom of cheek,
Nor radiant eye, nor skin as damask sleek,
Shall win a single wreath from hand of mine.

Nor mean my service, nor though chastened, cold;
To gaze unseen, unknown, wakes more delight,
Than misers feel when brooding o'er their gold.

Then the attempt to picture thee aright!
To shape thy absent form in fancy's mould!
Imagination takes no sweeter flight.

Passing th' enclosure where the dead repose,
I saw, in sable weeds, a gentle pair
Lingering with fond regard, at evening's close,
Beside a little grave fresh-swelling there:

Silent they stood, serene their thoughtful air;
There fell no tear, no vain complaint arose;
Faith seemed to prompt the unutterable pray'r,
And to their view the eternal home disclose.

Next Sabbath brought me where the floweret lay—
Record of high descent the marble bore,
Heir of a noble house, and only Stay;

And these words gathered from the Bible's store—
" The Lord hath given, the Lord hath ta'en away,
His holy name be blessed evermore."

X.

THEY tell me, Boy, that, with too eager pace,
I strain with thee up Learning's arduous steep,
And by untrodden paths advance, nor keep
The road, that gently rises from the base:

'Tis true, from height to height to loftier place,
I lead thee on, and barriers overleap,
Where others, by dull ways, obscurely creep,
Nothing beholding of the glorious chase;

Yet is thy watchful Father ever by,
Ever he stretches back a helping hand,
Informs thy steps, and bids thee fearless try;

One effort more, and on the top we stand,—
There, in the freshness of a purer sky,
Range we at leisure through the flowery land.

XI.

THEY picture Death a tyrant, gaunt and grim,
And, for his random aim, temper a dart
Of bite so mortal, that the fiery smart
Consumes, and turns to dust the stoutest limb.

Thus dire to meet, yet shrink not they from him
Who walk, by faith, in singleness of heart;
The simply wise, who choose the watchful part,
Nor let their eyelids close, or lamps grow dim.

Nor always dark, and terrible his mien;
As those, who by the couch the night-watch keep,
Have known, spectators of the blessed scene,

When friends, who stand around, joy more than weep,
As, with hushed step, and smile of love serene,
In the soft guise he comes of gentle Sleep.

CONSTANCE! though on the couch of sickness laid,
Thy present ill with pictures of the past
Is oft beguiled; so fresh the colours last
In thy mind's mirror pure, at will display'd;

For thou hast Alp and Apennine survey'd;
Rome on her ruined throne of empire vast;
Art's wonders, forms in mould of beauty cast,
And nature, lovelier than herself, portray'd.

Visions of Italy still charm thine eyes:
Often, amid the gloom of sleepless hours,
Thy chamber brightens with her happy skies;

Her fruits hang golden, fragrant breathe her flowers;
And tuneful, as the day in glory dies,
The knell of evening chimes from convent towers.

XIII.

Lord! I would hunger after that blest food,
Thirst after that life-giving draught of thine,
And ever, if to will and do were mine,
The one thing needful seek and only good;

But ah! to interrupt her better mood
How many Foes against my Soul combine;
Foes, that, unless thy powerful arm divine
Extend its aid, by me are ill withstood:

Yet rich thy Promise is, faithful thy Word—
" Ask, at my throne let all thy wants be told,
And in due season shall thy prayer be heard."

The prayer, thy grace now prompts, hear, Lord, at l
Deliver me, as thou wert wont of old,
And, in my weakness, glorify thy strength.

XIV.

Would I to healthful sounds reclaim my Lyre!
I pierce the green wood to some flowery nook,
There on sweet Spenser cast regardful look;
He chastens old, and kindles new desire.

Not more were wont the Muses to inspire
Dreamers of old with draught from sacred brook
Of Castaly, when strange emotions shook
Their tuneful souls, as winds the trembling wire.

From vain delights, and lap of slothful down,
Bewildered thoughts, and soft infectious speech,
Who would escape, must quit the impure town;

Returning, where, beneath the white-armed beech,
By valley's stream, or hillock's verdant crown,
Her simple lesson Nature waits to teach.

XV.

Roused by the billow's melancholy dirge,
I woke, as Night her sable banner furled;
What time pale mists, in forms fantastic curled,
Like spectral shapes, come flitting o'er the surge:

Then, looking eastward, on the ocean's verge
From the near sun I saw red flashes hurled;
As rolls the pageant from the nether world,
And from the waves the golden wheels emerge.

Never of old did more portentous light
Suspend the seaman's oar, when, like a pyre,
Lemnos appeared at evening, kindling bright;

Rather—when, tasked by Jove in sudden ire,
The God was labouring with his crew all night,
On glowing anvils shaping forked fire.

XVI.

EXPECTANT on the grass-crowned cliff we lay;
The signal sounded, to the enamoured wind
Three lovely barks their snowy sails unbind,
And big with swelling canvas stretch away.

Swans, on the bosom of calm inland bay,
That, by some fear to sudden speed inclin'd,
Urge the blue waters till they stream behind,
Not swifter seem, or whiter-winged than they.

Nor eager those, alone, who seek the prize;
As in full theatre, the scene begun,
Rank above rank attentive crowds arise:

Aloud the Victor, when the goal is won,
We greet, and with the vanquish'd sympathise;
Heedless, perchance, how our own race be run!

XVII.

I NEVER with such horror stood aghast,
As when in lone Pompeii's silent street,
I felt thy mighty pulse, Vesuvius, beat,
And from thy jaws saw burst the fiery blast:

Thunders were loud, and smoke in columns vast
Mantled the air with darkness, and strange heat
Warned the sad peasant from his vine-clad seat,
As down the fruitful slope the red stream pass'd.

I feared lest might return that deathful hour,
When to their Gods for help the people ran,
And there was none, in temple, nor in tower:

And to my vision came the enthusiast man,
Who perished in the breath of that foul shower,
Nature's dread secrets obstinate to scan.

XVIII.

Oft Winter, Babbicombe, thy lonely shore
Hath lashed, since, freighted with a laughing crew,
Our bark along the marge of Ocean flew,
And stirred with gentle keel thy pebbly floor:

We recked not what the future had in store,
Bright, as thy embayed waters, to our view
The present smiled, for life and hope were new,
And look of peace the far horizon wore.

Landed, in happy groups we wandered free,
Some ranged the woods, some 'thwart the deep blue air
Walked the high cliff, and traced a wider sea.

The rock our table formed, the turf our chair,
Nor sad the guests beneath the whispering tree,
For Youth and Innocence and Love were there.

XIX.

Friends, gentle Friends, how often I repeat
The wish, that near my own your dwelling stood,
Not proudly built, yet elegantly neat,
On some green slope, by hill o'erlooked and wood:

Thither I oft should turn my eager feet,
There with pure joys divert the pensive mood,
Nor idly trifle, precious time to cheat,
But prompt, and prompted be, to mutual good.

Happy, thrice happy those, who, ere their days
Be spent, from wandering in vain shadows cease,
And view serene, as fade life's evening rays,

The brightness of a better world increase;
Still onward led by Her, whose ways are ways
Of Pleasantness, and all whose paths are Peace.

XX.

Chief splendour of the azure-vaulted sky!
Thou from thy golden urn the softest ray
Dost pour, refreshing the sun-wearied eye,
And lighting fancy on her dreamy way:

Bewildered in the beautiful display,
Methinks that thou, and all the stars on high,
For me·alone usurp the throne of day,
So still and voiceless all earth's creatures lie:

Vain thought! how many commune with thee now,
On·sleepless couch, from out the prison's gloom,
Amid lone wilds, and on the distant prow.

Thou soothest those who weep beside the tomb,
And fond hearts at thine altar breathe the vow,
Dazzled with hope, and blind to future doom.

XXI.

HERE, where the night-breeze moans like a distant knell,
I would hold converse with my kindred dead,
And shape them to mine eye, as when they fled
To the pure clime where righteous spirits dwell:

Imagination work thy mightiest spell—
My Sire appears, light, such as sun-beams shed
On vernal showers, enwreathes his sainted head,
He seems to say—Son! guard thy Mother well.

Sisters! ye too do leave your heaven awhile,
For this brief moment surely were ye spared,
To teach me how above the Angels smile:

Brothers! with whom life's joys and pains were shared,
I mark the import of that warning style,
Lips never plainlier spake,—" BE THOU PREPARED."

XXII.

Past the grey tombs what space an arrow flies,
The darkening road winds down a hollow glade,
Romantic spot! and sweetly solemn made
By over-arching trees of giant size:

Above, Aricia's battlements arise,
As on the branches of the lofty shade
The town were based, with all its long parade
Of domes and turrets basking in the skies.

More shadowy depths and varied tints of green
Not Vallombrosa clothe, here, Stranger, stay,
And on thy tablet spread the sylvan scene:

Nor charmed alone the prospect's fair array,
Old memories my raptures flashed between,
And peopled thick the silent Appian Way.

XXIII.

Pacing, as I was wont, on day of rest,
Amid the Coliseum's awful round,
From distant corridor there came a sound,
As of a voice that published tidings blest:

Along the vaulted way I forward press'd,
And soon a group of dark-eyed Romans found,
Intent and fixed, like men some spell had bound,
The Preacher with such power their souls address'd.

The words he spake, his gesture, and rapt look,
Betokened one whom Heaven had rendered bold
To ope the treasures of the sacred book.

Methought the Shepherd visibly forsook
Temples, where holy things were bought and sold,
For two or three thus gathered to his fold.

XXIV.

Ere the wide waters on my view had smil'd,
From inland vale, in sunset's shapeful hue,
Oft Fancy traced their level line of blue,
And pictured cliffs where golden clouds were pil'd;

Often the Sea-birds' wail my mind beguil'd,
I loved the boisterous home from which they flew;
From out dark pines when winds loud murmurs drew,
Methought I heard the waves in chorus wild.

At length I blest a Brother's guiding hand,
The goal was reached, and as I stood entranced,
A new world viewing from the lofty land,

Sudden—around the precipice that veils
The western sky, a warrior-ship advanced,—
On the blue waste a Pyramid of Sails.

XXV.

Ye sacred Arks of Liberty! that float
Where Tamar's waters spread their bosom wide,
That seem, with towering stern and rampart side,
Like antique castles girt with shining moat;

Should War the signal give with brazen throat,
No more recumbent here in idle pride,
Your rapid prows would cleave the foaming tide,
And to the nations speak with thundering note.

Thus, in the firmament serene and deep,
When summer clouds the earth are hanging o'er,
And all their mighty masses seem asleep,

To execute heaven's wrath and judgments sore,
From their dark wombs the sudden lightnings leap,
And vengeful thunders peal from shore to shore.

XXVI.

Is this the spot where Rome's eternal foe
Into his snares the mighty legions drew,
Whence from the carnage, spiritless and few,
A remnant scarcely reached her gates of woe?

Is this the stream, thus gliding soft and slow,
That, from the gushing wounds of thousands, grew
So fierce a flood, that waves of crimson hue
Rushed on the bosom of the lake below?

The Mountains that gave back the battle-cry,
Are silent now, perchance, yon hillocks green
Mark where the bones of those old warriors lie.

Heaven never gladdened a more peaceful scene;
Never left softer breeze a fairer sky
To sport upon thy waters, Thrasymene!

XXVII.

Often, when standing fearful near the brink
Of towering cliff, whose rugged brow o'erhung
Some dark ravine, where solitary sprung
A lovely flower, wild rose, or glowing pink,

I've fondly gazed, until I ceased to shrink
From the sharp edge, and could myself have flung
To the low crevice, where the floweret clung,
Though with my prize I down were doomed to sink.

In this enchanting world of love and light
Are forms a thousand times more sweet and fair,
And precipices near, that more affright;

Taught by another's perilous proof, beware,
Nor lean too much on reason's vaunted might;
Those only are secure, who gaze not there.

XXVIII.

I STOOD at gaze where the free hills arise,
Whence rocks 'mid deepest solitudes are seen,
And glimmering through dark foliage, the blue sheen
Of Ocean stained with heaven's own sapphire dyes:

Then into the deep air I raised my eyes;
The stedfast dome was cloudless and serene,
Fit roof to over-arch so fair a scene,
For earth in loveliness vied with the skies.

Enrolled, methought, among a happier race,
I felt immortal moments as I said,
Death finds no entrance here, and Sin no place:

Then quick to mark where recent footsteps led,
I saw One bending o'er the furrow's trace,
And on his brow the primal sentence read.

XXIX.

My window 's open to the evening sky,
The solemn trees are fringed with golden light,
The lawn here shadowed lies, there kindles bright,
And cherished roses lift their incense high:

The punctual Thrush, on plane-tree warbling nigh,
With loud and luscious voice calls down the night;
Dim waters, flowing on with gentle might,
Between each pause are heard to murmur by.

The book that told of wars in holy land,
(Nor less than Tasso sounded in mine ears)
Escapes unheeded from my listless hand.

Poets, whom NATURE for her service rears,
Like Priests in her great temple minist'ring stand,
But in her glory fade when she appears.

BOLHAM, 1821.

XXX.

O Thou! whose golden reins curb steeds of fire,
Blest be the rosy Hours that onward bring
Thy glorious pomp, now Night with folded wing
Hides in her cave, and heaven's pale host retire:

Fresh from their flowery beds the gales respire,
To rapture new awakes each living thing,
Rivers run joyous, woods harmonious ring,
As Earth, unveiling, shows her green attire.

Now Ocean shines distinct, the bark unmoors;
Flocks to the dewy mountains from the fold
Go forth, the springing lark above them soars;

And hopeful Man, as on thy state is roll'd,
Welcomes the beam that o'er the cluster pours
A deeper dye, and ripens fruits of gold.

XXXI.

LIVED there beneath the earth in depths profound
A Race, like us, with reason's light endued,
Yet who, less privileged, had never viewed
The sky, the ocean, and the emerald ground;

Then were they sudden from these shades unbound,
And led into this world, with wonders strewed—
As they the spacious theatre reviewed,
How would the spectacle delight, confound!

The sun, the azure sky, the floating cloud,
The sea, woods, rivers, and the flowery sod,
And each fair scene the beams of day unshroud:

The star-pav'd heaven by shining planets trod—
With eyes in wonder rais'd, and rapture loud,
Ah! would they not exclaim? a GOD! a GOD!

XXXII.

TO THE REVEREND CARRINGTON LEY,
VICAR OF BERE REGIS, DORSET.

FRIEND of my youth! whom time hath made more dear,
Not evils, only, years, as they advance,
Darkly unfold, witness the happy chance!
That from such hateful distance brings thee near:

Scenes long o'ershadowed brightly reappear;
Again, perusing with enraptured glance
The early pages of life's sweet romance,
I taste the freshness of our vernal year.

Haste, my retreat hath store of charms for thee,
Sweet note of native birds, and by clear stream
Trees, whose green arches often cloister me;

Remembered books, awakening ancient theme,—
Nor wants there wine, laid up for sober glee,
When GRENVILLE was installed our Chief supreme.

XXXIII.

How oft maturer years are charmed with store
Of scenes from glowing pages caught in youth,
When words, like pictures, living colours wore,
And fiction's impress was as strong as truth;

The Red Sea! when the built-up waves down pour
On Egypt's host—amid the corn-sheaves, Ruth!—
Or, Cadmus, portrayed in profaner lore
Watching the growth of men from Dragon's tooth!

In my ideal gallery appear
Two trees, which I more fondly contemplate
Than any my own hands have planted here;

The Plane, that shaded Tully in debate,
And Fig-tree, to returning warriors dear,
That spread its branches near the Scæan gate.

XXXIV.

Columns, all statue-crowned, their deep files spread
On either hand, whilst from twin fountains spring
Waters, that beat the air with dewy wing,
Then radiant fall upon their marble bed:

To the majestic front thus proudly led,
What pencil's force, what strong imagining
Shall paint, as back the lofty gates they fling,
The firmament of glory overhead.

Fit emblem of the great Creator's deed,
When heaven's blue concave crowned the mighty plan,
And the first mortal earth's young verdure trod.

The Nations here, forgetful of their creed,
Exclaim—O noblest monument of man!
O Temple worthy of the living God!

XXXV.

I MAY not taste the fragrant breath of Spring,
And gaze upon her beauty, and caress
The flowers embosomed with such tenderness,
And her sweet advent not be heard to sing;

When insects are abroad on gentle wing,
And birds, melodious, throng the green recess,
When rising joys all living creatures bless,
And sounds of gladness through the valleys ring.

Now Earth 's redeemed from winter's icy chain,
And buds and blossoms drink the sun-lit shower,
And verdant fallows teem with infant grain,

I too would feel heaven's renovating power,
And on the true vine grafted, there remain
A living branch, until the vintage hour.

XXXVI.

DEATH! thou hast laid a matchless victim low
And overwhelmed, by such untimely doom,
The lordly hall and Peasant's bower in gloom,
So many hearts are pierced by this one blow!

Yet, blessed truth! though vanish'd from below,
Her beauty lives, her gentle virtues bloom
Imperishably fair beyond the tomb,
Where the pure streams of life for ever flow.

Adorned with every grace of form and mind,
She perfected what nature fondly plann'd,
And grew to be the model of her kind.

When worth, like hers, retires at Heaven's command,
To friend, or parent, grief is not confin'd,—
We mourn for dead a DAUGHTER OF THE LAND.

XXXVII.

The tidings came—my Brother was no more—
Heart-stricken, to the Palatine I went,
There on a sculptured stone Time's hand had rent,
I sat me down my spirit to restore:

Friends there were none, They wept on Albion's shore;
Yet each grey Fane, each aged Monument,
Seemed on my sorrow feelingly intent:
Such look of sympathy the Ruins wore.

And Men, with whose high deeds the world yet rings,
Appeared, as evening gloomed, and Conquerors pass'd
With Nations in their train, and captive Kings;

And voices, from that shadowy concourse vast,
Whispering the vanity of earthly things
Were heard, as flitted by the midnight blast.

Rome, 1822.

XXXVIII.

Louisa! guarding still the name of Winn,
Rememberest thou Devonia's vernal hue,
Her orchards blooming flowery vales within,
Her dewy skies, and sea of softest blue?

Rememberest Greenway, and th' expanding view
Of Dart's full waters, Becky's thundering din,
And northward, where, oak-garlanded anew,
Down from her mountain-lair career'd the Linn?

That valley too, strange wilderness of stone,
And the bold path hung midway from the surge,
And sky-built crags, old Druids' misty throne—

These scenes remembered, I too may emerge
Who gazed with thee, however dimly shown,
Content, if seen within the picture's verge.

XXXIX.

'Twas near the walls that gird th' imperial town,
Where from a lonely Convent's still retreat
I saw, whilst Tiber glowed beneath my feet,
From heaven's illumined vault the Sun go down;

The lofty Capitol, like burnished crown,
Blazed on the City's brow,—each hallowed seat,
Each mournful relic of the perished Great,
Seemed once more brightening into old renown;

The Plain in purple haze lay slumbering deep,
The giant arches, that bestrode it, shone
A bridge of gold to blue Albano's steep.

Man, here alas! for ages overthrown,
With no gleam kindles, sunk in deathlike sleep,
His ruin, ROME, is darker than thine own.

XL.

A SPOT, whose beauty ev'n from gainful haste
Wins brief delay, long space enjoyed by those
Who the slow walk repeat, or in repose
Eye the blue waves, and sea-born breezes taste:

Green swelling hills of Devon, foliage-traced,
With cliffs romantic round bright waters close—
Here blushes early, lingers late the rose,
The myrtle here survives the leafy waste.

Like isles pine-pinnacled the glassy deep
O'ershadowing, when War's loud note alarms,
Here England's battle-ships dread muster keep:

The Peasant oft, so glory's service charms,
Viewing the bannered squadrons from this steep,
Joins the bold crew and dares the strife of arms.

XLI.

Season of bursting leaves! for many a day
I've watched thy coming, and strict search have made
Beside the tangled copse, and open glade,
For the fresh charm of new-invested spray:

Blest dropping clouds! mild warmth of brighter ray!
At length the chestnut from the brown wood's shade
Flings emerald gleams, along the lane's arcade
Elms with green light illuminate my way:

Yon Oak, where build the social birds and pair,
Into rich foliage is swarming out,
And sunward shineth with a golden glare.

Ye tardy trees, that linger still and doubt,
Unbind your leafy locks, the southern air
Invites, and stranger cuckoo's mellow shout.

XLII.

As One, who in the battle's hot career
Sees a loved comrade fall, yet onward goes
Urged by the rapid war, and whelming foes,
And, scarcely sighing, o'er him drops no tear;

Thus I, when Death a brother struck, was near,
Yet in such dread array came on fresh woes,
That desperate borne to meet th' impending blows,
Scarce a wild look I cast on one so dear.

Now hath misfortune spent her angry store,
And slow-recovering from the stunning shock
At length the prostrate senses wake once more;

Feeling returns, with deep remembrance sore
Of treasure lost, upon the lonely rock
I sit, and shipwrecked hopes and life deplore.

January, 1826.

XLIII.

THE gale that winged with fragrance softly blew,
Now spread the sulphurous taint of death,—the rill
Tuneful and clear, was bloodstain'd now and still,—
Banks trodden down, and blacken'd their green hue;

Yet to this stream from adverse camps withdrew,
To quench hot thirst, Warriors, with peaceful will;
Rancour was soothed, and Pity's tender thrill
Kindled in each rough breast emotions new.

Like Knights of old, at close of battle fray,
Each to the other courteous service lends,
And hands are joined and vows exchanged that day:

Sudden a voice of loud command ascends,
'To arms,' 'to arms,'—the battle moves, and they,
Who strangers smote before, now smite their friends.

XLIV.

O YE! who through the vale of sorrow plod,
Attend the words which Israel's prince declared,
When God was wrath, nor his own servant spared,
Till deep repentance won the approving nod.

Yes—when we bend beneath affliction's rod,
No more by beauty of the world ensnared,
Vain Man at sight of coming judgment scared,
Turns from his idols to the living GOD.

Though pain excruciate, and death affright,
Yet as the wasted body sinks, the soul
Beholds eternal things with purer sight.

Affliction! so my wandering steps control,
That, tho' I pass with thee through darkest night, .
I may at dawning reach the heavenly goal.

XLV.

How silently on her smooth axle turns
Th' unwearied Earth, bearing with rapid ease
Waters of mighty rivers and broad seas,
Whilst not a drop o'erflows their brimming urns!

Naught hindered when the loud volcano burns;
Alike unmoved by hurricane or breeze;
Perish her infant flowers, or, aged trees,
Bent on her errand all delay she spurns:

By night, by day, still eager to fulfil
Her task of ages, in a ceaseless round
She moves, obedient to her Maker's will.

Ah would that Man, on his brief journey bound,
So kept his course, and, spite of transient ill,
Thus unperturb'd a Traveller were found!

XLVI.

SHE grieved that her loved Season's pensive hue,
Its colours sadly gay, so soon should fade,
And she not seek, in thoughtful mood, the glade,
Nor from grey steep the mellow landscape view:

Others too grieved, that One, so fond and true,
Marked not with them each sudden gleam and shade,
The leaf's·light fall, the stillness—deeper made
By rustling breeze, or birds forlorn and few.

O pure delight! when minds are well agreed,
To commune thus with WOMAN, early taught
In Nature's page devotedly to read:

Lady, with *thee*—who, in thy vernal hour,
Like some heaven-favoured plant, art richly fraught
With Wisdom's golden fruit, and Beauty's flower.

Had I the skill of Lawrence and chaste hues,
Then would I, Lady, thy resemblance trace,
And oft before mine eyes the portrait place,
Nor trust alone to Memory and the Muse;

Then others might thy countenance peruse,
And say, when bending o'er th' expressive face,—
To paint that tender look's peculiar grace
The fondest words were vain that Poets use!

Ah me! for neither Art brings full content,
Since—thy mild voice—how were its sweetness told?
And how—thy manner's gentle blandishment?

Woman, thus precious, Genius' sons of old
In visions saw, heaven-taught to represent
Her, whose fond arms the holy babe enfold.

XLVIII.

Raise, raise, dear gentle Flower, thy drooping head,
That gracious Heaven may open to thy view,
Cheer with its beams, refresh thee with its dew;
Look up, dear gentle Flower, be comforted:

Set in His garden, by His bounty fed,
Whilst others by the way-side idly grew,
In purer air, among the chosen few,
Thou hast in strength and beauty flourished.

'Ah, say, how droop not, if, in that same bower,
A loved one sink beneath such early doom,
That grew with me in sunshine, and in shower.'

Ere the full fragrance, and immortal bloom
Of that fair world be Hers, dear weeping Flower,
Thy loved One must be gathered to the tomb.

XLIX.

Proud One! I reckon thee thus highly placed
At the Great Master's hospitable board,
For other purpose than to wear and waste,—
He claims thy service, claims to be adored:

This homage paid, 'tis given thee to taste,
To see o'er all thy works his blessing pour'd;
Whilst those, who only to their pleasures haste,
Shall pine amid th' abundance of their hoard.

' Ah, say, how serve him best, how best adore'—
A Brother, Sister see in all who grieve,
And in thine own behold a common store:

Who doeth thus shall thankfully believe
His words, who all our sins and sorrows bore,—
More blessed 'tis to give than to receive.

L.

Oh never, LADY, in the desert plain
Did Pilgrim hail with such intense delight
Green shade and fountain cool, as I the sight
Of one whose friendship was my earliest gain:

Blooming I left thee, 'mid the virgin train,
Like some fair rose on stem of graceful height,
Whose beauties open to the flattering light,
Of golden morn, and skies without a stain.

Alas! not mine alone the saddened brow;
Thine too with sorrow's cloud is overcast,
And eyes that beamed with joy, are tearful now:

Ah! let us hope that every storm is past,
That voyaging abreast with gentle prow,
We may the peaceful haven reach at last..

LI.

TIME, I rejoice, amid the ruin wide
That peoples thy dark empire, to behold
Shores against which thy waves in vain have roll'd,
Where man's proud works still frown above thy tide.

The deep-based Pyramids still turn aside
Thy wasteful current, vigorously old
Lucania's temples their array unfold,
Pillar, and Portico, in simple pride.

Nor less my joy, when, sheltered from thy storms
In earth's fond breast, hid treasure bursts the sod,—
Elaborate stone in sculpture's matchless forms.

Oft did I mock thee, Spoiler, as I trod
The glowing courts where still the Goddess warms,
And stern in beauty stands the quivered God.

LII.

WELL I remember, on my youthful ear
When first the solemn Hallelujahs fell;
Through dim aisles roll'd the echoes, like the swell
Of mighty waters when the winds career:

Great was my transport, and sublimed by fear;
High thoughts of those, who in God's presence dwell,
Possess'd my soul, and Judgment, Heaven, and Hell
As dread realities did now appear:

And when the deep notes ceas'd, and evening gleamed,
A voice serene amid the pillared gloom
Of the Redeemer sang, and the Redeemed;

Of Death, and Resurrection from the tomb;
How the rejected ONE, and the blasphemed,
Should in His glory come, and seal our doom.